# *StarGate*

from the screenplay and novelization by

DEAN DEVLIN &
ROLAND EMMERICH

adapted by

SHEILA BLACK

Level 3

Retold by David Wharry
Series Editors: Andy Hopkins and Jocelyn Potter

**Pearson Education Limited**
Edinburgh Gate, Harlow,
Essex CM20 2JE, England
and Associated Companies throughout the world.

ISBN: 978-1-4058-8204-0

First published in Great Britain by Puffin Books 1995
This adaptation first published by Penguin Books Ltd 1996
Published by Addison Wesley Longman Ltd and Penguin Books Ltd 1998
New edition first published 1999
This edition first published 2008

3 5 7 9 10 8 6 4 2



Typeset by Graphicraft Ltd, Hong Kong
Set in 11/14pt Bembo
Printed in China
SWTC/02



Published by Pearson Education Ltd in association with
Penguin Books Ltd, both companies being subsidiaries of Pearson Plc

# *Contents*

# Introduction

*Daniel shut his eyes, walked into a wall of light, and suddenly saw himself flying among the stars, millions of them. He seemed to fly for thousands of years, until . . .*

The StarGate is hidden under the sands of Egypt for ten thousand years. Then, in 1928, some archeologists find it. There is strange writing on it, which they can't fully understand.

Sixty years later, in America, the United States Army are interested in the StarGate. A young archeologist, Daniel Jackson, discovers the meaning of the writing on the StarGate. It says: 'A MILLION YEARS INTO THE SKY IS RA, SUN GOD.' Then he finds a way to open the StarGate.

What is on the other side? Daniel and some soldiers go through the gate to find out. They come to another world millions of light years from Earth. There, Ra, the Egyptian Sun God, is king. But his people are not free – they are his prisoners.

Ra must kill the visitors from Earth and close the StarGate for ever. Daniel and the soldiers must fight Ra to stay alive, and then find a way home. But then Daniel meets Sha'uri. She is beautiful and he loves her. Perhaps he will never go home.

*StarGate* is a film by Roland Emmerich. It was one of the most popular films in America in 1994. Since then, there have been three long-running television *StarGates*: *StarGate SG-1*, *StarGate Atlantis* and *StarGate Universe*.

People have been interested in the life of the Egyptians for thousands of years – their gods, their writing and their pyramids. The biggest pyramids are at Giza, just outside Cairo. The largest one is that of the Pharaoh Khufu. It was built over 4500 years ago and is also called the Great Pyramid. The pyramid in StarGate looks like Khufu's pyramid.

## Chapter 1 8000 BC

The boy painted the animal on the wall of the cave. He could see it hiding in the grass. He moved closer. Outside, men did the same, knowing the boy could see the animal with his eyes that always burned with a strange, cold fire. The boy said the animal's name, 'Khet!', hit the painting, and the real animal fell dead, killed by a stone. The men lifted their arms and shouted the boy's name, 'Ra!'

That night, everyone dressed as animals and danced. Ra never danced with them. He never laughed or played. People said he was born without a heart.

Nobody saw a dark shape cross the sky. Ra had a strange feeling and looked up, but it was already gone. Later, as everyone slept under the stars, a strong wind came and a light, as bright as the sun, shone in the sky. Everyone ran to the cave except Ra. He walked towards the light, smiling, feeling happy for the first time.

## Chapter 2 Cairo, Egypt, 1928

The car left Cairo on the road to Giza. Catherine Langford sat in the back with her father, an archeologist. She was only nine but he was already teaching her the writing of the Egyptians. He was going to see his friend Ed Taylor. Eight years ago he and Ed found some writing in the pyramid of Ti. It said someone hid a 'mysterious and terrible thing' near the pyramid. Ed and her father searched for years. Other archeologists said they were wasting their time. Then, that morning, Ed phoned from Giza. 'We've found something!' was all he said.

The car stopped in the desert by a large hole. Workers were trying to lift something out of the ground. Ed was studying old Egyptian writing on a large stone. There were thirty-nine unknown letters in a circle on it. In the middle there was a group of six of the unknown letters. Ed pointed to some writing underneath. 'It says *a thousand years . . . the stars*, something like that, then . . . *Ra, the sun god . . .*'

The workers were lifting a large stone ring, about five metres wide, out of the ground. Catherine followed Ed and her father down into the hole. She saw the same mysterious writing round the ring. 'It's made of an unknown kind of stone,' Ed said. Catherine noticed something gold shining on the ground by the ring. She picked it up. It was a small *udjat* eye, half-man's, half-bird's, the eye of the god Ra. Quickly, she put it in her pocket.

The workers were shouting, frightened by something under the ring. Catherine went closer and saw shapes like a broken hand, and a strange head, like a dog's, burnt into a piece of stone. And she immediately thought of Anubis, the dog-headed god of the Dead.

## Chapter 3 Los Angeles, Sixty Years Later

Daniel cleaned his thick glasses while Doctor Ajami, his old teacher, spoke to the meeting of the world's top archeologists. 'Please welcome Daniel Jackson, our youngest Doctor of Archeology – he is not yet thirty. He speaks eleven dead languages and I'm sure you've all read his most . . . interesting ideas on Egypt.'

Daniel knew that nobody agreed with these ideas. He got up to speak and heard Rauchenburg, a world-famous archeologist, say, 'The boy needs to see a doctor.'

When the room was quiet, Daniel said, 'Men made the first cars over a hundred years ago. Do you agree that we make better ones today, Doctor Rauchenburg?'

*Daniel cleaned his thick glasses while Doctor Ajami, his old teacher, spoke to the meeting of the world's top archeologists.*

'Er . . . yes, of course,' Rauchenburg replied, a little uncomfortable.

'Yes,' Daniel said. 'We make things much better today than, say, three thousand years ago, don't we? So why, then, didn't the science and language of the Egyptians change for three thousand years? And why, at the beginning of that time, did their writing suddenly change from cave paintings to a full written language?'

People were talking openly now. 'What are you trying to say?' Rauchenburg asked.

'Khufu's pyramid, the greatest of all the pyramids, is another example,' Daniel went on.

'An example of what?' someone said. 'Please explain.'

'Of course,' Daniel replied. 'Every pyramid but Khufu's is full of writing. There isn't a word or a date anywhere on it. So, can we really be sure the Egyptians built it?'

People laughed loudly. Some were already leaving. An old woman got up at the back. 'Most interesting, Doctor Jackson. And perfectly right. So, who do *you* think built it?'

'I have no idea who built it,' Daniel replied. 'Or why.'

'Maybe it was little green men from Mars,' someone said.

Everyone was leaving. Doctor Ajami came over to Daniel, angry. 'Why did you bring up that stupid idea, Daniel? You'll never find a job anywhere now. Goodbye!'

Daniel walked home thinking about Ajami's last words. There were more bills in his letter box. Upstairs, the door of his flat was open. He ran in, hoping to catch a robber. Instead he saw the old woman from the meeting looking at unpaid bills on his desk. 'Hey!' he shouted. 'How did you get in here?'

She smiled. 'My name is Catherine Langford. I've come to offer you a job, Daniel. With the Army.'

He laughed. 'The Army! Are you trying to be funny?'

'No. You have no job, no money, and after today no

*'My name is Catherine Langford. I've come to offer you a job, Daniel. With the Army.'*

university will ever give you work again. But that isn't why you'll say yes. You'll say yes to show that your – our – ideas are right.' She gave Daniel some photographs. His mouth fell open when he saw the stone. She put an aeroplane ticket on his desk and left.

## Chapter 4 Top Secret

High in the Rocky Mountains, the car left the road and stopped at a gate. The driver showed papers to a soldier, drove on into the forest and stopped outside a cave. Ten soldiers were guarding it. The biggest said, 'Pleased to meet you, Doctor Jackson. I'm Lieutenant Colonel Kawalsky. Follow me.' They went into a small metal room inside the cave. The door closed and the room went down . . .

Underground, Kawalsky took Daniel into a room the size of a church. In the middle, Catherine Langford was waiting next to the stone. She smiled and said, 'I've shown photographs of the unknown signs in the circle to some of the archeologists who were at your talk – and nobody can understand them.' Daniel listened while she read out the known signs inside the ring.

Daniel smiled. 'No, no.' He pointed to a group of signs. 'Here, it really says *a million years into the sky is Ra, sun god*. And, here, the last word isn't *door into the night* but *StarGate*.'

'The stone, is ten thousand years old,' Kawalsky said.

'Impossible!' Daniel replied. 'The earliest Egyptian—'

'The Army's scientists never make mistakes,' a man behind them said. They turned. 'I'm Colonel O'Neil, from General West's office,' said a hard-looking soldier at the door. His cold blue eyes studied Daniel. 'Doctor Jackson, you are here to help Doctor Langford tell us what the signs round the ring mean. I must warn you that everything here is a secret of the United States Army.'

Daniel started immediately, working day and night, trying every idea that came into his head. On the third night he went outside to get some fresh air and to talk to Kawalsky, who was reading a newspaper. Daniel looked over his shoulder to see what he was reading – it was the part of the paper about star signs. He suddenly realized: the shape made by the stars above him in the sky was very like the shape of one of the signs in the newspaper, Orion. He hurried back underground, found a photograph of an Egyptian painting of the night sky... and saw immediately: the unknown signs were groups of stars!

## Chapter 5 The Seventh Sign

General West came into the room, followed by O'Neil and a line of soldiers. 'Okay,' he said, 'Let's hear, Jackson.'

Daniel pointed to a photograph of the stone. 'The signs round the outside ring are groups of stars. So, the group of six signs in the middle probably mean a place, a kind of address. I'll explain. If a place isn't on the ground but in the air, then to know where it is we need to know three lines that meet in that place. Each line must have two ends – so, six places. See?'

'Six isn't enough,' O'Neil said. 'To go to a place in the... air, you need a seventh place – to start from.'

'Of course,' Daniel replied. He pointed to a small picture next to the six signs: the sun shining on a pyramid. 'Here it is. In Egyptian, the sign of a pyramid means "Earth".'

'He did it!' Catherine shouted. 'You'll have to show him the ring now.'

'Show me what ring?' Daniel asked.

Minutes later, deeper underground, they went into a cave bigger

*'There's your "StarGate",' Catherine said to Daniel.*

than a football field. The beautiful stone ring shone like silver in the middle of lines of computers and machines. 'There's your "StarGate",' Catherine said to Daniel.

'What is that strange white stone?' Daniel asked.

'Nobody knows. It's harder than anything on Earth.'

'Okay, let's see if Jackson's right,' West said to a scientist at a computer. A machine moved the seven signs round the ring. 'Stop!' said the scientist, watching the computer. When the last sign came to its place, there was a sudden noise, like a strange music. Seven lines of light began to shine from the white stones towards the middle of the circle. A circle of light began to grow where the seven lines met. The circle of light grew until the stone ring was full of it. 'Quick, send our machine into it!' West shouted. The scientist started a strange-looking machine on wheels. It moved slowly into the circle of light and disappeared. 'Where's the machine? Where's it gone?' West shouted.

The scientist was watching another computer. 'The machine is already several light-years from Earth. It's going towards the Cirrian group of stars.'

Catherine threw her arms round Daniel. 'You see: a *StarGate*, a gate to the stars! You've done it!'

O'Neil joined them. 'You've done your job, Jackson. Go home now – and don't forget this is top secret.' He went to watch the computers.

Daniel ran after him. 'You can't keep *this* secret!'

'Who needs to know?' O'Neil replied coldly.

Suddenly, Daniel understood. 'And *you're* going to go through the StarGate, aren't you?' O'Neil said nothing. 'Take me and Doctor Langford with you, O'Neil, please!'

'We don't need archeologists now, Jackson.'

'Come and look at this!' West shouted. 'The machine's camera is sending pictures back to Earth.'

They saw a stone wall and part of another StarGate.

'The signs on it are different,' O'Neil said.

'The machine says the air there is the same as Earth's,' said the General. 'But I won't send men over there if I'm not sure they can get home again. You'll have to go too now, Jackson – to read those signs. You will leave tomorrow at 06:00 hours.'

## Chapter 6 Through the StarGate

The time was 05:44. Daniel, O'Neil, Kawalsky and three other soldiers, Feretti, Brown and Porro, stood waiting with boxes full of things they needed. Catherine put her gold *udjat* eye round Daniel's neck. 'This will bring you luck,' she said. At 05:45, the scientist began to move the white stone signs. When the seventh sign came to its place, seven lines of light shone into the middle of the ring and a ball of bright light grew and filled the circle.

They pushed the boxes through the StarGate first. O'Neil seemed to be the only one who wasn't frightened. He was the first to walk into the circle of light and disappear. Kawalsky ordered Feretti, Brown and Porro to go next. 'I'll see you soon, Jackson – I hope,' Kawalsky said before he went through.

Daniel shut his eyes, walked into the wall of light, and suddenly saw himself flying among stars, millions of them. He seemed to fly for thousands of years, until . . . someone shook him. It was Kawalsky. He went and shook the others. Like Daniel, they weren't hurt. They lay next to another StarGate, in a large, dark room with walls of shiny black stone. 'Let's go!' said O'Neil. Brown opened a box, took out lamps, then they went into a much larger room. It was more beautiful than anything Daniel knew on Earth, but he had a strange feeling that he already knew this place . . . They went through more dark, empty rooms, then outside into bright sunlight. Daniel saw three suns

*O'Neil was the first to walk into the circle of light and disappear.*

shining in a deep blue sky, and an endless sea of sand. He looked round. They were standing at the bottom of a pyramid. Daniel looked up at it and knew now why he felt that he already knew the rooms inside. The pyramid was the same as Khufu's pyramid on Earth.

## Chapter 7 The Bomb

Near the pyramid, they stood at the top of a sand hill. O'Neil, looked round with field glasses and saw only desert. 'There's nothing here but the pyramid. It's time to go home.'

'We can't,' Daniel said. 'First, we have to find the seven signs, the address. On Earth it was on a different stone.'

'I told you to search inside the pyramid,' O'Neil said.

'I did. And it's empty. There isn't a single sign on it – just like Khufu's pyramid on Earth.' He looked round at the sea of sand. 'Now where do we search?'

Kawalsky picked Daniel up by his shirt. 'Listen you little rat, you make that StarGate work or I'll break your neck!'

'Be quiet Kawalsky,' O'Neil said and thought for a few seconds. 'Okay, let's put the tents up by the pyramid.'

They went back to the StarGate room and took some of the boxes outside. While the soldiers were putting the tents up, O'Neil went back alone to the StarGate room and opened another box. He opened a secret door at the bottom of it and took out the pieces of a bomb. He put the bomb together, put an orange key in his pocket, and went outside again.

While O'Neil and the others put up the tents, Daniel went to the top of a sand hill. He noticed shapes in the sand, like a horse's feet, but much larger. He followed them to the top of another sand hill, and saw a strange animal looking at him. It was the size of a small lorry and had long, dirty hair. He went nearer. The animal smelt

*While O'Neil and the others put up the tents, Daniel went to the top of a sand hill.*

terrible but it seemed friendly. It went down on its knees and ate some chocolate from Daniel's hand. O'Neil, Kawalsky and Brown ran over the hill pointing their guns. 'Don't shoot!' Daniel shouted. Frightened, the animal ran away.

## Chapter 8 'Little Bit'

They ran after the animal until, at the top of a sand hill, they suddenly stopped. They were looking down into a deep, narrow valley. Thousands of men, women and children were mining white stone in it. They had dark skin and wore dirty clothes. One of them saw the soldiers and cried out. Thousands of eyes suddenly looked up. O'Neil told his men not to point their guns and to follow him down. 'I want you to try to talk to them, Jackson,' he said.

'Um . . . hello?' Jackson said to the first miner. 'I'm Daniel.' The man smiled, but seemed to be frightened. He suddenly pointed to the *udjat* eye round Daniel's neck. '*Naturru ya ya!*' he screamed wildly, dropping to his knees and putting his face in the sand. Thousands of miners below did the same.

'I said speak to them, not frighten them,' O'Neil said.

An old man in red clothes and two young women came to Daniel. One of the women, who was very beautiful, offered him water. The old man pointed, smiling. 'He's asking us to go somewhere with him,' Daniel said to O'Neil.

They left the valley with the old man, followed by thousands of miners. Daniel asked questions in Egyptian but the man didn't understand. All Daniel learned was the animals' name – they were *mastadges* – and that the old man's name was Kasuf.

Kasuf, who was head of the miners, was not sure if the strangers were really gods. But he hoped they were, because their arrival stopped the mining and this meant that his people were in trouble.

*The old man pointed, smiling. 'He's asking us to go somewhere with him,' Daniel said to O'Neil.*

His son, Skaara, who looked after the *mastadges*, walked next to him. The beautiful young woman, who was Skaara's sister, walked next to Daniel. He couldn't keep his eyes off her. She looked like an Egyptian goddess, he thought.

The smelly *mastadge* put its nose in Daniel's pocket, looking for chocolate. 'Only a little bit,' Daniel said, giving it some. Skaara laughed and said, '*Little bit . . .*'

'Hmm . . . not a bad name for a smelly thing,' Daniel thought. Then, miles away, he saw the walls of a city.

## Chapter 9 The Sand Storm

The gates of the city opened and they went through narrow streets to a square. Kasuf showed Daniel a large *udjat* eye, the Eye of Ra, the Sun God, on a wall and everyone went down on their knees. 'They probably think Ra sent us,' Daniel said. The sky grew suddenly darker and people began hurrying from the square. Something was wrong. Daniel, O'Neil, Kawalsky and Brown ran to the city's gates and saw a dark cloud over the desert. 'It's a sand storm,' O'Neil said. 'It's over the pyramid and it's coming this way.'

Miles away, Feretti and Porro ran through the flying sand to the pyramid. Inside, Feretti tried the radio but it didn't work because of the storm. They heard a strange noise above the sound of the storm, and when the pyramid began to shake they thought the earth was moving. They couldn't see the golden, pyramid-shaped star-ship landing on the pyramid they were in. It came down to sit perfectly on top. Deep inside the pyramid below, in the great room next to the StarGate room, a blue light began to grow inside a stone circle on the floor. Seconds later, Feretti heard something behind him. He turned and saw someone much larger than him . . . with the head of a dog.

## Chapter 10   The Goddess in White

After the sand storm they ate in the square with Kasuf and other heads of the city. Daniel was trying to talk to Kasuf when his daughter brought them fruit. She smiled at him and suddenly he knew he was in love. Looking into her dark eyes, like the *udjat* eye, he remembered the first Egyptian sentence that he ever learned. He put his finger in water and wrote it on the table: *Ra came from the sky*. When Kasuf saw the writing he got up, frightened. Quickly, he took Daniel away through the streets.

Later, Daniel lay on a bed, washed, smelling nice, wearing clean white clothes. He heard women's voices outside the room. The beautiful young woman came in, alone, wearing white clothes like his. She looked frightened and Daniel suddenly understood: they were giving her to him to be his wife. 'Please,' he said, 'I really like you, you're very beautiful, but . . .' He opened the door.

Kasuf and other heads of the city were waiting outside. '*Khha shima nelay?*' Kasuf said angrily. The young woman began to cry. Daniel smiled uncomfortably.

'I . . . er . . . just wanted to say thanks for . . . my beautiful new wife. Goodnight now.' He pulled her inside. 'Please, don't cry. Stay here if you want. I'm Daniel.'

'Dan-yur,' she said slowly and pointed at herself. 'Sha'uri.' He repeated her name and she smiled.

'We came from the pyramid,' he said.

When he made the sign of a pyramid on the floor Sha'uri put her hands over her eyes, frightened. The gods killed anybody who tried to write. Her people had no written language. And so nobody knew the story of their people. If Dan-yur is a god he will kill me just for looking at writing, she thought. But was he really a god? Her people were prisoners of gods, and this man didn't speak to her like a god to a prisoner . . . She made a line on

*She made a line on top of the pyramid, then a circle. It was the only sign that she knew, and Daniel saw immediately what it was. It was the sign for Earth.*

top of the pyramid, then a circle. It was the only sign that she knew, and Daniel saw immediately what it was. It was the sign for Earth.

Sha'uri took Daniel secretly to a building. They went down some stairs, deep underground, and she opened a door. Inside a small, empty room, she pointed at the stone wall. Daniel saw the same sign for Earth, which also meant Ra, the sun god. It was the only writing in the room. Daniel felt the sign, pressed it, and they jumped with surprise when a secret door opened. They saw writing all over the walls inside, and as soon as Daniel saw it he was sure: Sha'uri's language *was* almost the same as Egyptian. The writing told the story of war against animal-headed gods. There were pictures of Anubis, the dog-headed god, pushing people through a StarGate and making them travel across the sky to another world . . . Daniel asked Sha'uri about a picture of a pyramid shining in the sky. A boy stood below it, lifting his arms to the light.

'I see you've learnt to speak their language,' said O'Neil, behind them. He was standing at the door with Kawalsky, Brown and the boy, Skaara.

'How did you find us?' Daniel said.

'The boy showed the *mastadge* your jacket. It smelled it and came here. What do the pictures say, Jackson?'

'They tell a story that began ten thousand years ago. A traveller escaped from a world where he was weak and dying. He searched the stars, looking for a way to live longer. Look, here it says he came to *a world rich with life* – Earth – and *changed his body into the shape of their people* – us! – *so that he could live until the end of time.* He took the body of a boy, called himself Ra, the Sun God, and brought thousands of prisoners here through the StarGate to mine *the wonderful white stone.* Then there was trouble. Once, while he was here, people on Earth killed Ra's guard and hid the StarGate under the ground, so he couldn't return. Ra did not

*'The seventh one – the address of* this *world – will be at the bottom, here,' said Daniel, pushing away some sand until he saw. . . The bottom was broken into hundreds of pieces.*

want his prisoners here to know anything. He didn't want them to know the true story about him. So he stopped all reading and writing.'

While Daniel was talking, Kawalsky saw part of a stone in the floor. 'Maybe this is what we're looking for,' he said.

It was.

The stone was just like the one that Ed Taylor found at Giza. And all six signs in the middle were the same as the ones on the StarGate in the pyramid. 'The seventh one – the address of *this* world – will be at the bottom, here,' said Daniel, pushing away some sand until he saw... The bottom was broken into hundreds of pieces.

'The StarGate will never work without that seventh sign,' O'Neil said. 'We're going back to the pyramid now, before those suns come up!'

## Chapter 11 The Blue Light

O'Neil, Kawalsky, Brown and Daniel left the city without noticing that Skaara was following them on Little Bit. Soon they saw the golden pyramid sitting on top of the stone one. 'It's the star-ship!' Daniel said. 'Remember the pictures in the room?' O'Neil felt the key to the bomb in his pocket. He had secret orders to use it if they found danger to Earth – and that star-ship looked like big danger! When they came closer they saw the tents, broken by the sand storm. 'I'm going inside,' O'Neil said. 'Jackson, you come with me. Kawalsky, Brown, stay here.'

Inside, O'Neil and Daniel saw Feretti's hat next to the radio, then they heard shouts. They hid quickly and watched a large man with the head of Horus, the Egyptian bird-god, walk past. His clothes were metal and he carried a long, straight weapon with a piece of the shining white stone at its end. When the bird-man was gone they hurried to the StarGate room. O'Neil gave Daniel his gun. 'Watch behind us,' he said. He quickly opened the secret part of the box . . . and saw that the bomb was not there.

Suddenly, two Horus men were standing at the door. Between them was a much bigger man, with the head of the dog-god, Anubis. He came towards them, pointing his strange weapon, his metal clothes shining. Daniel was so frightened he dropped O'Neil's gun. The dog-man pushed Daniel and O'Neil into the next room and into the circle of white stone on the floor. Immediately, a strange blue light began to grow inside the circle, and the next thing Daniel knew, he and O'Neil were standing in a different room.

They saw a golden chair, shining with white stones. A golden statue of Ra sat in it. Children dressed in gold stood near the statue. The statue's face was like the masks of the dead kings of old Egypt. Above the chair was a golden circle with the *udjat* eye, the Eye of Ra. The eyes of the mask were the same, but so real that they seemed to be looking at them. Then the statue got up. It was alive!

Ra's mask smiled at the prisoners. More children came in, carrying pieces of the bomb. They put them down in front of O'Neil. Daniel didn't know what they were.

Anubis touched a shining stone on his throat and his dog's mask opened to show a man's head inside. Daniel noticed that the Sun God's skin wasn't gold now but light brown, and his mask was opening too. Inside was the face of a handsome young man, about twenty years old.

He pointed at O'Neil and said in Egyptian, 'Kill him.'

Daniel saw Anubis point his weapon at O'Neil and jumped to stop him. A line of light shot from the white stone on the weapon's end. Daniel felt something hit his heart, then everything went black. Another line of light shot from the weapon and O'Neil fell to the

*The dog-man pushed Daniel and O'Neil into the circle of white stone on the floor. Immediately, a strange blue light began to grow inside the circle.*

floor. Ra smiled. 'And have you killed all the other Earth men, sweet Anubis?'

'Yes, Great God from the Sun. These two make six.'

Ra smiled and pointed to O'Neil's body. 'Take that away and put it with the others.' He went to Daniel's body and saw something that didn't please him. His smooth brown hand went down and angrily pulled Catherine's *udjat* eye from Daniel's neck.

## Chapter 12 Only One Ra

Skaara searched in the sand near the tents and found a box. He opened it and saw guns inside. He pulled the box behind a sand hill. Little Bit was waiting there. While he was tying the weapons on the *mastadge's* back, he saw a door open in the side of the star-ship. Three aeroplanes, like Horus birds, flew out carrying bombs. A minute later, when he was leaving, Skaara saw clouds of black smoke coming from the city.

Near the city's gates, one of the Horus bombers came out of the smoke, flying low over Skaara. The pilot studied Little Bit and the boy carefully and flew away only when he was sure that Skaara was returning from the mine.

Inside the city, houses were burning everywhere. The streets were full of the dead. Skaara saw his sister, Sha'uri, busy helping people. 'Where's Dan-yur?' she asked. Skaara was sure that Daniel was dead, but he said he didn't know. She turned away, crying.

♦

A large stone coffin lay in a room in the star-ship. Its heavy stone top slowly opened. Daniel's body lay inside. The hole in his heart was gone. His eyes opened. And Daniel sat up, reborn.

*A large stone coffin lay in a room in the star-ship. Its heavy stone top slowly opened. Daniel's body lay inside.*

Minutes later, he followed a child into a room with a pool. Ra got out of it, young and handsome, not looking like someone ten thousand years old.

'I died?' Daniel said in Sha'uri's language.

'I can mend your bodies so easily,' Ra said. He smiled and pointed at some pieces of the bomb on a table. 'Your world has changed much since I left. Now you have the science to make a bomb that can kill many thousands of people in a few seconds. But you still don't understand the science of my wonderful white stone!' His golden eyes shone suddenly. 'You were wrong to open the StarGate! I will send your stupid bomb back to Earth, made a thousand times stronger with one small piece of my white stone. Thousands of years ago I went to your world. I was millions of light-years away from home, searching for another body to live in. I was dying. My people were dying. I took the body of a young boy and made myself into a god. It was so easy – Earth people are so stupid! I gave you science, a language, everything. And now it is time for me to take them away again. I am going to end your world!'

'Then why am I alive again?' Daniel asked.

'I have a body like yours, but I'm not like you inside. I have no love, no kindness. You are alive again because I must show my people again that there is only one god, one Ra. Tomorrow, in front of the miners, you will kill your soldier friends for me.'

## Chapter 13 To Know Is to Be Strong

Sha'uri was sure that Daniel was dead. After dark, she went to the secret room and cried for hours. Skaara came and she dried her eyes, knowing that she had to tell him the hidden story of their people. She explained the pictures to him and, like his sister, he understood that Ra was not born in the sun, that he wasn't a god. He felt suddenly strong. He wasn't frightened of Ra now. His people didn't have to live as Ra's prisoners . . .

When the three suns came up, a Horus guard came to the city. 'Take Ra's people to the House of their God,' he ordered Kasuf. An hour later, thousands of people were waiting outside the pyramid. They watched two Horus guards push out O'Neil, Kawalsky and Brown and knock them to their knees. Then Anubis came out, pulling Daniel by the arm. Sha'uri's heart jumped when she saw him, and Skaara began to move closer through the crowd.

Everybody shouted 'Ra!' as the golden boy-god came outside. He sat down in his golden chair and Anubis walked over to Daniel. The crowd was sure that the dog-god wanted to kill him. Skaara was trying hard to make Daniel notice him. There wasn't much time . . .

Anubis put his weapon in Daniel's hands and pointed at O'Neil, Kawalsky and Brown. Something in the crowd shone in Daniel's eyes. He saw Skaara using a piece of glass to shine sunlight at him. Skaara opened his coat, and showed the gun hidden inside. Daniel showed Skaara he understood, then shouted, 'Great Ra orders me to kill my brothers!' He pointed the weapon at O'Neil, but instead of shooting him, he turned suddenly and shot at Ra.

O'Neil jumped up, hit a Horus guard, took his weapon and shot at Ra too. Skaara did the same. But Ra was already inside the pyramid. O'Neil killed both Horus guards with his weapon, but more guards were coming at him. Anubis took another weapon and shot at the soldiers. He looked round for Daniel and O'Neil but couldn't see them. He guessed that they were hiding among the miners. He called a pilot and told him to go out and search the crowd. Another sand storm was coming so they had to be quick.

*As the sand storm came nearer, a shadow like a bird moved slowly over the frightened crowd.*

As the sand storm came nearer, a shadow like a bird moved slowly over the frightened crowd. The pilot looked down at every face, until he saw a *mastadge* running away into the sand storm, carrying people on its back . . .

Minutes later, Ra called the pilot to his room. 'We lost them in the storm, Great Ra,' the pilot said.

Ra smiled and put a small ring of the white stone round his hand. The ring began to shine. 'Don't be afraid,' he said, his hand coming up to touch the pilot's head. For a few seconds, the man shone brightly, shaking, screaming, before he turned into nothing.

## Chapter 14 Nowhere to Run

Daniel, Sha'uri, O'Neil, Skaara and the soldiers fought through the flying sand, following Little Bit up a hill into a cave. As soon as they were inside, Daniel said, 'Why didn't you tell anybody about the bomb, O'Neil?'

'My orders are to send you home, then to search for any possible danger to Earth. If I find any, I have to blow up the StarGate. Well, guess what? I found danger, a lot of it!'

'The bomb is Ra's now,' Daniel said. 'Tomorrow he's going to send it back to Earth, a thousand times stronger.'

'He told you this?' O'Neil said uneasily.

'Listen,' Daniel said. 'The real danger is not the bomb here but the StarGate on Earth. As long as it's working, he can always go there. We have to close it again, for ever!'

O'Neil laughed. 'Very clever, Jackson. But thanks to you, we can't, can we? All we can do is wait for this storm to stop and try to plan what to do next – any ideas?'

♦

When Daniel woke up the next morning, Sha'uri came to him and O'Neil. 'Skaara has a idea,' she said. 'Today is one of the special days when we take the white stone to the House of Ra and send it away through the StarGate. We can hide in the bags of stone.'

Later, Daniel saw Skaara painting a pyramid on the wall of the cave. When he painted three suns above it, Daniel jumped up and joined the suns and the pyramid into a shape. 'Look!' he shouted. 'That's the seventh sign.'

## Chapter 15 Countdown

The miners left the mine with their *mastadges*, going towards the pyramid. They were so frightened of the Horus guards that only one guard was with thousands of miners. A man fell down in the heat. The guard came over to hit him. Suddenly, the miner turned over and shot the guard dead. It was O'Neil. Daniel and Skaara pulled guns from their miner's clothes. 'Stop!' Kasuf shouted. 'The Sun God will be angry again!' The other miners, who were as frightened as Kasuf, didn't know what to do.

Daniel pressed a stone on the dead guard's mask. It opened to show a man's face. 'Is this a god?' he shouted. 'Look, he's like you!' Everywhere, miners began talking: if the guard wasn't a god, then maybe Ra wasn't either . . .

Soon the miners arrived at the pyramid. Ra watched the long line of people from a window. He was sure that the Earth men were among them. He called Anubis. 'Take the bomb to the StarGate room. If the Earth men get inside, kill them all again and send their bomb to Earth.'

Outside the pyramid, Skaara ordered everyone to go down on their knees. He sang the usual song, 'Ra who comes from the sun, we bring you your white stone!' Three Horus guards searched the

*Ra watched the long line of people from a window.*

bag on the first *mastadge's* back. Daniel and O'Neil, hidden inside, jumped out and shot them dead. Immediately, the stone door of the pyramid began to close, but not fast enough. O'Neil, Daniel and Sha'uri jumped inside just before it closed.

They ran to the StarGate room. The bomb was in pieces on a table. Daniel pushed the first sign round to its place then saw O'Neil putting the bomb back together. 'What are you doing?' he said. 'It's the StarGate on Earth that we must close.'

'That's *your* job, Jackson. I'm staying here to finish mine.' He pushed the orange key into the bomb's lock and turned it. A clock began counting down: 12:00, 11:59, 11:58, 11:57 . . . He put the key back in his pocket. 'Jackson, you have twelve minutes to work the StarGate. Take the girl with you if you want to.'

Suddenly, the room was full of white light and Sha'uri fell down. A Horus guard was shooting his weapon from the door. Daniel shot him, then ran to Sha'uri. She was dead. He put his arms round her. 'Get up!' O'Neil shouted. 'You've got to go through the StarGate. Now!'

Daniel noticed blue light in the circle in the next room – and suddenly remembered the coffin. He lifted Sha'uri's body and ran into the light. 'No, wait!' O'Neil shouted, but it was too late. He saw that part of Sha'uri's dress, which was outside the circle, was lying on the floor after she and Daniel disappeared. O'Neil heard something, looked round and saw Anubis. The dog-man knocked O'Neil across the room then ran to him. On his feet again, O'Neil hit him as hard as he could and ran towards the bomb. He had to stop it to give Daniel time to get back . . .

♦

Inside the star-ship, Daniel hurried to the coffin and put Sha'uri in it. He watched the stone top close softly over her. When he looked

*O'Neil hit Anubis as hard as he could and ran towards the bomb.*

up he saw Ra in the room, his golden skin shining. Too frightened to move, Daniel watched him come nearer. The coffin opened and Daniel saw Sha'uri, alive, sleeping. 'Wonderful!' Ra said. 'Now you can both die again – together.'

♦

In the pyramid below, Anubis ran to O'Neil and knocked his arm away before he could put the key back into the bomb's lock. The key went flying into a dark corner. O'Neil pulled Anubis's metal arm up behind his back and broke it. 'Bad dog!' O'Neil said, kicking the metal mask. The big man fell and lay still. Again, O'Neil noticed the piece of Sha'uri's dress next to the circle in the next room – and he had an idea. Quickly, he pulled Anubis to the circle and left him with his head inside it. The blue light began to shine inside the circle while O'Neil ran to look for the key. In the StarGate room, he looked at the clock: 7:39, 7:38 . . .

♦

In the star-ship, Daniel picked up Sha'uri and carried her into the room with the golden chair. He noticed the white stone circle filling with blue light. He stood in the centre of the circle. Ra smiled. 'This will be the great Anubis, "God of the Dead". He has killed your friends and sent your bomb back to your world. And now I will kill both of you.' Ra lifted his hand. The shining white ring was round it. Light shot from it and knocked Daniel down. Ra came nearer, put his hand into the circle and touched Daniel's head with the ring.

The stone's terrible white fire burned brighter and brighter inside Daniel's head. Seeing the blue light growing brighter, Daniel suddenly remembered how it cut through Sha'uri's dress. Forgetting the burning fire in his head, he took Ra's arm and held the burning ring on his head. Ra didn't understand: why

*Forgetting the burning fire in his head, he took Ra's arm and held the burning ring on his head.*

did the stupid man want to do this? Did he want to die more quickly?

Ra saw the blue light growing brighter and tried to pull his hand out of the circle. 'Let go!' he shouted. But Daniel held on. The room was swimming round him now. All he could see was Catherine's *udjat* eye round Ra's neck. He caught it in one hand and pulled hard. The last thing he saw was the blue light cutting cleanly through Ra's arm . . . Then everything went black.

Ra stood by the circle, holding his arm and screaming for help. The blue light in the circle grew brighter, and suddenly, in place of Daniel, lay the head of Ra's terrible killer, Anubis.

Ra knew he had to get to the coffin. It could grow back his lost arm . . . And he knew that he had to escape: the miners knew now that he wasn't a god. He could hear the angry crowd outside. A line of blood followed him to the golden chair. He touched a white stone on the chair's arm, and the star-ship's machines started.

## Chapter 16 00:03, 00:02, 00:01 . . .

At last O'Neil found the key. He ran to the bomb, put the key in the lock, turned it. And nothing happened. *01:09, 01:08, 01:07 . . .* The clock kept on counting down! Why didn't it stop? He could feel the pyramid shaking. What was happening? He noticed blue light in the next room and saw Sha'uri and Daniel lying in the circle.

Daniel woke up, looked round and saw Sha'uri waking up too. They were both alive! He saw Ra's cut-off hand lying in the circle in a pool of blood and felt the pyramid shaking. Ra was leaving . . . Then he suddenly remembered the bomb. He looked into the StarGate room and saw O'Neil busy with it. He could see the bright red numbers counting down: *00:22, 00:21,*

*00:20* . . . He helped Sha'uri to her feet and they ran to O'Neil. 'Turn it off!' he shouted, 'Can't you hear the star-ship? Ra's leaving!'

'Don't you understand?' O'Neil shouted. 'I can't! The Army put a special one-way lock on it and they didn't tell me! It won't stop!'

'Then I have an idea,' said Daniel. 'Quick, help me!'

He picked up the bomb and put it in the circle of light . . .

♦

Inside the star-ship, Ra waited for the machines to lift the star-ship off the pyramid. Out of the corner of his eye, he saw something in the white circle: the bomb! He saw the red numbers counting down: *00:02, 00:01* . . . and he knew it was too late.

Outside, the crowd watched the star-ship lift off the pyramid. 'He's leaving, father!' Skaara shouted to Kasuf 'We're free at last!'

Inside, Daniel, Sha'uri and O'Neil hurried to the pyramid's entrance. It was still closed. Daniel saw a small circle of white stone on the wall, pressed it and the great door slowly opened. The crowd screamed with happiness when they saw Daniel, O'Neil and Sha'uri come out. Kasuf and Skaara pointed up above them.

They watched the star-ship fly higher and higher. 'He's going,' Daniel said to O'Neil.

Suddenly the star-ship turned into a great white ball of fire in the sky. 'And he's never coming back,' O'Neil replied.

Kasuf came to Daniel. 'For thousands of years we were his prisoners,' the old man said. 'Now, thanks to Dan-yur, he is only a cloud of smoke.' He lifted Daniel's arm in the air and thousands of miners shouted their thanks.

♦

*O'Neil said, 'Goodbye.' Quickly, without looking back, he walked into the pool of light and was gone.*

An hour later, thousands of people went to the StarGate room to watch the Earth men leave. Daniel turned the signs round the great stone ring. When he pushed the last sign into place, the seven lines of light shone into the middle. O'Neil watched the shining pool of light grow into a great white ball, then he turned to Daniel and said, 'You first, Jackson?'

'No, I'm staying here, O'Neil,' Daniel said, putting his arm round Sha'uri.

Daniel saw the soldier smile for the first time. 'Good luck to all the family,' O'Neil said, and shook hands with Daniel, Sha'uri, Skaara and Kasuf.

'Come and visit us when you want,' Daniel answered. 'It's not far – only a few million light-years away. And give Catherine this.' He gave O'Neil the *udjat* eye. 'Tell her it brought us luck.'

'We needed it,' O'Neil said. 'Goodbye.' Quickly, without looking back, he walked into the pool of light and was gone. The soldiers quickly followed him. The light inside the ring disappeared and the StarGate stopped. And Daniel, Sha'uri, Skaara, Kasuf and their people left the pyramid and began the long walk back to the city.

# ACTIVITIES

## Chapters 1–4

*Before you read*

**1** Discuss these questions with other students.

**a** The picture on the front of this book shows a pyramid with a circle round it. On the circle there are some signs. Behind it are the stars. What do you think the book is about?

**b** What do you know about Egypt? Where is it? What famous things are there? What do you know about the country's history, people and writing?

**2** Look at the Word List at the back of this book. Find any new words in your dictionary. Then answer these questions.

**a** Which two things on the list are under the ground?

**b** Which words are titles for important army officers?

**3** Which of these words goes in each space below?

archeologist desert god mask statue weapon

In the **(a)** ..... an **(b)** ..... found a very old **(c)** ..... of an Egyptian **(d)** ..... . Its face was covered by a **(e)** ..... . It held a long knife as a **(f)** ..... .

**4** Read the Introduction to the book. Are these sentences right or wrong?

**a** The StarGate is about 100 years old.

**b** It is a gate to another world.

**c** The ruler of that world, Ra, was known in Egypt a long time ago.

**d** The story in this book is from a television programme.

*While you read*

**5** Put these sentences in the right order. Write 1–7.

**a** Daniel finds the meaning of the signs round the ring. .....

**b** Catherine Langford finds a small *udjat* eye in Egypt. .....

**c** Ra walks towards the bright shape in the sky. .....

**d** Daniel goes to the Rocky Mountains. .....

**e** Catherine Langford offers Daniel a job with the US Army. .....

**f** Daniel tells some important archeologists that the Egyptians did not build the Great Pyramid of Khufu. .....

**g** Catherine's father and his friend find a large stone ring near the pyramid. .....

*After you read*

**6** Who does each thing a–g? Choose from this list.

Ra Catherine Langford Ed Taylor

Doctor Ajami Doctor Rauchenburg

Lieutenant Colonel Kawalsky Colonel O'Neil

**a** ... has cold eyes and never laughs or plays.

**b** ... finds some writing on a stone.

**c** ... teaches Daniel archeology.

**d** ... says Daniel needs to see a doctor.

**e** ... gives Daniel an aeroplane ticket.

**f** ... meets Daniel outside a cave.

**g** ... works in General West's office.

**7** Work with another student. Have this conversation.

*Student A*: You are Daniel. You don't think the Egyptians built Khufu's pyramid. You are not sure, but you think that perhaps it was people from the stars.

*Student B*: You are Rauchenburg. You think the Egyptians built Khufu's pyramid. You also think that Daniel's ideas are crazy.

## Chapters 5–7

*Before you read*

**8** Look at the pictures in Chapters 5–7. Which of these do you think will happen?

**a** Daniel will build a StarGate.

**b** Catherine will find the StarGate.

**c** Daniel will go through the StarGate.

**d** Some soldiers will go through the StarGate.

**e** Daniel will travel to Egypt.

**f** Daniel will travel millions of miles from Earth.

*While you read*

**9** In which order do we read about these things? Write the numbers 1–12.

| | | | | | |
|---|---|---|---|---|---|
| **a** | a stone ring | ..... | **g** | the Egyptian sign for Earth | ..... |
| **b** | a gold *udjat* eye | ..... | **h** | a sand hill | ..... |
| **c** | a strange animal | ..... | **i** | seven lines of light | ..... |
| **d** | another StarGate | ..... | **j** | millions of stars | ..... |
| **e** | chocolate | ..... | **k** | a large cave | ..... |
| **f** | a bomb | ..... | **l** | three suns | ..... |

*After you read*

**10** Why are these things important to the story?

**a** the Egyptian sign of a pyramid
**b** a white stone ring
**c** a machine on wheels
**d** the Cirrian group of stars
**e** the signs on the second StarGate
**f** an orange key

**11** Work with another student. Have this conversation.

*Student A*: You are Daniel. Tell a friend about what you saw when you first walked through the StarGate. Tell your friend how you felt.

*Student B*: You are Daniel's friend. Ask him questions about his adventure. What did he see? How did he feel?

**Chapters 8–10**

*Before you read*

**12** Daniel and the others have just arrived on a world far away from Earth. What do you think they will find there? Which of these things are most possible?

an airport  a city  a king
a mountain  a sand storm  a secret door
a star-ship  grass  miners

*While you read*

**13** Who says these words? Who to?

**a** '*Naturru ya ya!*'

........................ to ........................

**b** 'I said speak to them, not frighten them.'

........................ to ........................

**c** '*Little bit ...*'

........................ to ........................

**d** 'It's over the pyramid and it's coming this way.'

........................ to ........................

**e** 'I really like you, you're very beautiful, but ...'

........................ to ........................

**f** 'Dan-yur.'

........................ to ........................

**g** 'I see you've learnt to speak their language.'

........................ to ........................

**h** 'Maybe this is what we're looking for.'

........................ to ........................

*After you read*

**14** Why are these things important in the story?

**a** the *udjat* eye **b** white clothes **c** a secret door **d** Daniel's jacket **e** the seventh sign on the stone

**15** Put these words in the right sentences.

cloud fruit gods guns light
nose prisoners square valley

**a** They were looking down into a deep, narrow ..... .
**b** O'Neil told his men not to point their ..... .
**c** The smelly *mastadge* put its ..... in Daniel's pocket.
**d** They went through narrow streets to a ..... .
**e** Daniel saw a dark ..... over the desert.
**f** Deep inside the pyramid a blue ..... began to grow.
**g** Kasuf's daughter brought them ..... .
**h** The ..... killed anyone who tried to write.
**i** Ra brought ..... to mine the white stone.

## Chapters 11–13

*Before you read*

**16** What will happen next? In these sentences, one of the words in *italics* is right. Talk to another student. Decide which word is probably right.

- **a** O'Neil has secret orders to use a *bomb / gun*.
- **b** Anubis opens his dog's mask. Inside is the face of a *dog / man*.
- **c** Skaara opens a box. There are *guns / radios* inside.
- **d** Aeroplanes drop *bombs / food* on the city.
- **e** Sha'uri understands that Ra was not born in the *sun / moon*.

*While you read*

**17** Draw lines between the words on the left and the right to make correct sentences about the story.

| | | |
|---|---|---|
| **a** | O'Neil | kills the pilot. |
| **b** | Skaara | shoots at the soldiers. |
| **c** | Daniel | gives Daniel his gun. |
| **d** | Sha'uri | lies inside a large stone coffin. |
| **e** | Anubis | doesn't find Daniel and O'Neil. |
| **f** | The pilot | goes to the secret room and cries. |
| **g** | Ra | ties weapons on Little Bit's back. |

*After you read*

**18** What happens first? What happens next? Put these sentences in the correct order.

- **a** Daniel shoots at Ra.
- **b** O'Neil looks for the bomb.
- **c** Anubis kills Daniel and O'Neil.
- **d** Three aeroplanes drop bombs on the city.
- **e** Daniel and O'Neil hide among the miners.
- **f** Ra takes the *udjat* eye from Daniel.
- **g** Daniel and O'Neil meet Ra.
- **h** Ra mends Daniel's body.

**19** Which colour a–d goes with which word on the right?

| | |
|---|---|
| **a** black | light |
| **b** blue | skin |
| **c** brown | smoke |
| **d** white | stone |

## Chapters 14–16

*Before you read*

**20** Look at the last picture in the book. Discuss these questions.

- **a** Where do you think the people are?
- **b** Who do you think is walking through the StarGate?
- **c** Do you think Daniel and Sha'uri will go through the StarGate too? Why (not)?

*While you read*

**21** Are these sentences right (✓) or wrong (✗)?

- **a** Little Bit follows Daniel into the cave. .....
- **b** O'Neil wants to blow up the StarGate. .....
- **c** Ra is going to send the bomb back to Earth. .....
- **d** Daniel paints a pyramid on the wall of the cave. .....
- **e** The miners kill a Horus guard. .....
- **f** O'Neil, Daniel and Sha'uri go inside the pyramid. .....
- **g** Daniel puts the bomb back together. .....
- **h** A Horus guard kills Sha'uri. .....
- **i** O'Neil breaks Anubis's arm. .....
- **j** Daniel hurts Ra. .....
- **k** O'Neil turns the bomb off. .....
- **l** The star-ship blows up and Ra dies. .....

*After you read*

**22** Daniel decides to stay with Sha'uri. Work with another student. Have this conversation.

*Student A*: You are Sha'uri. Daniel's life here will be very different from Earth. Also, you don't speak his language and he doesn't speak yours. You are worried.

*Student B*: You are Sha'uri's brother. You like Daniel. You think he will be a good husband. You also think he can help your people. Tell Sha'uri your opinion.

**23** How do you think these people feel at the end of the story? Why?
O'Neil   Catherine Langford   Doctor Ajami
Doctor Rauchenburg   Kasuf   General West

**Writing**

**24** Find and write some interesting facts about the pyramids of Egypt and the old Egyptian gods.

**25** At the beginning of the story, Daniel doesn't think that the Egyptians built Khufu's pyramid. He doesn't know who built it, but he has some ideas. Write a conversation between him and a friend who doesn't agree with him.

**26** O'Neil has orders to search for any possible danger to Earth. If he finds any danger, he must blow up the StarGate, and he has a bomb for this. But later Ra tries to send the bomb back to Earth. Do you think it was a good idea to give O'Neil a bomb? Say why.

**27** You are going to go through the StarGate and travel to another world. You can take ten things with you. Think about how you will live on the other world and the possible dangers and problems. Write a list of ten things that you will take. For each thing, say why you are taking it.

**28** Write a short description of three of these people: Daniel, O'Neil, Ra, Sha'uri, Anubis. Write about what they look like, what they do and their good and bad sides.

**29** After Ra dies, Daniel decides to stay with Sha'uri in her world. Write about his first week after the others have gone back to Earth.

**30** You are Daniel. You have learned the language of this new world. You are talking to Kasuf. He asks you about life on Earth. He has many questions. He wants to know how people live and how things are different. Write your conversation with him.

**31** You are Ra. For thousands of years you have watched people on Earth. You have seen many new ideas and ways to live. Write about the changes since you lived on Earth.

**32** Have you seen the film of this book? If you have, which did you like better – the film or the book? Why? If you haven't seen *StarGate*, have you seen a science fiction film like it? Write about the film.

**33** Some people love science fiction books and films like *StarGate*, and some people hate them. What do you think of them and why? Compare them with other kinds of book or film.

## WORD LIST

**among** (adv) in a group of

**archeologist** (n) a person who looks for old things under the ground and studies them. This science is called **archeology**

**army** (n) a country's soldiers for fighting on land

**BC** Before Christ or before year 0

**blow up** (v) to destroy something, using a bomb

**bomb** (n) a thing that blows up and destroys things and kills people

**cave** (n) a large hole in a rock wall or under the ground

**coffin** (n) a box where a dead person is put

**Colonel** (n) a title for a soldier with a lot of officers and men under him

**desert** (n) a very dry area with few or no living things

**god** (n) a great being who is above the natural world

**Lieutenant Colonel** (n) an important soldier just under a Colonel (See *Colonel* above).

**mask** (n) a thing that hides or protects your face

**mine** (n/v) a hole in the ground where **miners** look for gold or other useful metals

**pyramid** (n) a shape with four sides that come to a point at the top

**reborn** (adj) born again

**statue** (n) a man-made metal or stone copy of a person

***udjat*** (n) an old Egyptian word meaning the eye of the god Horus

**waste** (n) to fail to use something well

**weapon** (n) any thing that a person uses to fight or to kill people

## The Island of Dr Moreau

*H. G. Wells*

Edward Prendick is travelling in the South Pacific when his ship goes down. He is saved after many days at sea by another ship, and a passenger, Montgomery, nurses him back to health. Prendick becomes interested in the mystery of Montgomery's life. Why does he live on an unknown Pacific island? Why is he taking animals there? And should Prendick fear the dark secrets of Montgomery's master – the even more mysterious Doctor Moreau?

## The Fugitive

*J. M. Dillard*

One night a man kills Dr Richard Kimble's wife. It was a man with one arm, but the police believe it was Kimble who murdered her. He escapes from the police and goes searching for his wife's killer. But Detective Gerard is looking for Kimble too and wants him dead or alive . . . *The Fugitive* is a big Hollywood film starring Harrison Ford and Tommy Lee Jones.

## Dr Jekyll and Mr Hyde

*Robert Louis Stevenson*

Why is the frightening Mr Hyde a friend of the nice Dr Jekyll? Who is the evil little man? And why does he seem to have power over the doctor? After a terrible murder, everyone is looking for Mr Hyde. But he has disappeared. Or has he?